You Belong Here

CELEBRATING THE
SINGLE WOMAN'S PLACE
IN THE FAMILY OF GOD

ANTENESHIA SANDERS

You Belong Here: Celebrating the Single Woman's Place in the Family of God

The Daily Grace Co.® exists to equip disciples to know and love God and His Word by creating beautiful, theologically rich, and accessible resources so that God may be glorified and the gospel made known.

Designed in the United States of America and printed in China.

Living in your *identity*
as a member of the
family of God should
change the way
you *experience* life
as a single person.

Table of Contents

How to Use This Resource

You Belong Here: Celebrating the Single Woman's Place in the Family of God is meant to remind you of your place in the family of God. As single women, we might sometimes find ourselves wondering where we belong—and if that belonging even exists for us. Amid all the questions and uncertainty we feel because of our singleness, we may wonder if there is significance for us in our churches and in the family of God.

Friend, there is a place for you here. There is belonging for you here. Jesus Christ went to great lengths to purchase your place in the family of God. Jesus has gifted you with the ability to bless His body—the Church—and to edify the people of God.

Our hope for this resource is that you would be able to use it alongside your Scripture reading and prayer time. In the pages that follow, you will find poems and prayers for meditation, stories of women in the Bible who found belonging in the family of God, and words of encouragement and truth built around intentionally chosen passages from Scripture. Read through this resource as slowly as you need to, as many times as you need to. Allow it to guide your prayers and your meditations as you receive what this book has to offer you in this season.

We pray that you come away blessed, strengthened, and encouraged with a profound knowing that *you belong here.*

Jesus Christ went to *great lengths* to *purchase your place* in the *family* of God.

May belonging meet you right where you are.

Opening Blessing

May belonging meet you
right where you are.

And loose every lonely thought

Free you from the fear of "what if . . ."

And sever all notions of seclusion.

For Jesus is near.

And through Him you come to the Father

Who has established a kin-
dred that never ends

Who intends your thriving in
His holy temple of saints

And your participation in
this family of priests.

May you know that love is already yours.

May you know that "alone"
is not all that there is.

May you take your place in a
much grander genealogy

Than mere romance could
ever bring about.

May you know that you belong here.

Living in your identity as a member of the family of God should *change the way you experience life* as a single person.

Our Heavenly Father

MATTHEW 6:8–13

A variety of past experiences may have brought you to this season in your life. Whether you have been single all your life or you are newly single as a result of a divorce, you can probably relate to many of the sentiments that come with being unmarried. Often, singleness can feel isolating and lonely. If you are unmarried or without a family of your own, you may feel like you are floating through life untethered. You may bear the weight of broken family relationships along with the reality of being single. You may wonder if you are invisible or if anyone really cares about what is going on in your life. Even if you are perfectly content in your singleness, maybe you desire a little reassurance. However it is that you find yourself single, take comfort in this truth:

You have a heavenly Father. Because you have a heavenly Father, you belong to His family — a family you join when you place your faith in Christ, accepting Him as your Savior.

Living in your identity as a member of the family of God should change the way you experience life as a single person. You do not have to do it alone. He has offered us a home and a family, and desires for us to experience all the benefits of belonging. One of these benefits is being able to call on our heavenly Father in prayer, together with other believers.

In Matthew 6, Jesus teaches His disciples how to pray in what is traditionally called the Lord's Prayer. When Jesus taught His disciples to pray, He invited them to use a personal and familial name for the King of heaven. It is the same name that Jesus Himself uses for God — "Father." The Lord's Prayer is not only a model for how to approach God but is also an intimate means of relating to Him. To God the Father we can bear our hearts and present our deepest desires.

If marriage is what we long for, we can safely ask our Father. If we need provision, God hears our petition. If we need peace, He comes near and comforts us. We can ask for whatever it is we need. The One who sits high in the heavens beckons His children to call on Him. In fact, we find in the Lord's Prayer a communal cry meant to unite all of God's children:

"Our Father . . ."

"Give us . . ."

"Deliver us . . ."

As we pray, we are reminded that we are citizens of God's kingdom, single or not. Though His kingdom is a heavenly one, He desires to bring it near to us. He is the One who knows fully what His children need before they form the words in their mouths to ask. Our Father in heaven asks us to call on Him, not just for His own glory but for our benefit as well. As we draw from the words of the Lord's Prayer, we know that He is able to save us from temptation and protect us from evil. We know that our Father is eager to forgive, giving us the ability and desire to also offer forgiveness to others. In whatever season of life we find ourselves in—even in singleness—our Father is there with us.

Life as a child of God is meant to be lived in community. So, if you feel alone and unseen, remember you are not. There is One who knows you through and through, and you are part of His family. He longs to be known by you and to be your guide and companion through this life. Though your desire for a husband may be great, know that the Lord holds you closer (Isaiah 41:10), loves you more (Romans 8:37–39), and is the most constant companion (Hebrews 13:5)—more so than anyone else, even the most God-fearing husband. In your singleness, God is a good Father—a perfect Father. He has created for Himself a global family, and you are part of it. If you are wondering where you belong, you belong right here.

> God is a *good* Father—
> a *perfect* Father.

He has created for Himself
a global *family*,
and *you* are part of it.

Reflection

Do you ever feel "untethered?" How does it encourage you to know that you have a heavenly Father?

How does the communal nature of the Lord's Prayer change the way you think about singleness?

He is a God who *woos* through *sunsets*
and *mountain ranges* and *oceans*.

The Family of God

JOHN 3:1–4, JOHN 1:12–13

Those who place their faith in Jesus are born again into the family of God. Belonging to God's family frees you to shift your focus from finding a spouse to enjoying relationship with God and community with His people. In a world that tries to convince us that we are only as good as our romantic relationships, we can take comfort in the God who pursues and desires us more than any human ever will, knowing that we can only be truly satisfied in right relationship with Him.

He is a God who woos through sunsets and mountain ranges and oceans. He is a God who beckons us to Himself by revealing His nature through His Son, Jesus Christ. While salvation does not erase your desires, it does give you a new perspective from which to view them. The only relationship status that defines you is your relationship with God the Father, the Son He sent, and the Spirit indwelling all those who believe.

What are the requirements of belonging to God's family? Scripture tells us that God's children are the ones who have received His Son, Jesus. In John 3, the Jewish leader, Nicodemus, approaches Jesus in the night, having heard about His teachings and signs (John 3:1–2). Jesus explains to him that only those who are born again can enter the kingdom of God.

Nicodemus, perplexed, wonders how someone could physically be born again. Jesus replies, "Truly I tell you, unless someone is born of water and the Spirit, he cannot enter the kingdom of God. Whatever is born of the flesh is flesh, and whatever is born of the Spirit is spirit" (John 3:5–6). If we have a relationship with Jesus, we are children of God—a right given to those who place their faith in Christ, and it changes everything (John 1:12).

In His kindness, God made a way for us to be His children. Maybe you have a habit of defining yourself by your lack of marriage or a romantic relationship.

But understand: *you are not your singleness.*

"Unmarried," "widowed," and "divorced" are merely adjectives—not identities. Jesus carried our sin on the cross that we might enter into a new family—His family. In His love, He has taken away the shame of our past—whatever that may be—by bearing that shame on the cross. If you have received Jesus, you can be sure that you have been born again into His family. You are defined by your connection to God through Jesus Christ.

Maybe past failures have brought you to where you are today in this season of singleness. A previous relationship might have ended specifically because of something you did. You may be carrying the heaviness of sexual sin or wishing you had not crossed a certain boundary. Take comfort. You are not the sum of your mistakes.

Disregard the notion that you can never shake your past. The family of God is made up of the broken and the sinful—those who have come to Jesus for forgiveness and rest. Just as Jesus told Nicodemus, no one who believes in the Son will be condemned (John 3:18). If you have been born again, you are not marked by your missteps but by Jesus's sacrifice on your behalf.

Or maybe this is not you. Maybe you have yet to place your faith in Jesus. There is no better time than now to receive the right to be called a child of God. He longs to give you new life and new fellowship with Him. In Him is a companionship that far eclipses all others. You can be free from the pressure of finding "true love" and connection. The invitation to belong has been extended to you. You can be born again—into God's family.

For more on what it means to be born again, see "What Is the Gospel?" on page 163.

You are defined by your *connection to God through Jesus Christ.*

The *invitation* to belong has been *extended* to *you.*

Reflection

Do you feel like you wear your singleness as an identity?

In addition to giving you His Son, how has God "wooed" you? How has He tangibly shown you His love?

God's love for you existed
long before you did and has been
waiting for you all of your life.

Loved

ROMANS 8:35–39, JOHN 3:16

What will separate you from the love of God? Shall loneliness or heartache? Even if these feelings accompany your waking every morning, know that in comparison to God's love, they are mere shadows. God's love for you existed long before you did and has been waiting for you all of your life. While the world tells you that you must earn its affection, God never will. Trying to make God love you more is like trying to make water more wet. It is like trying to find a spot on the shoreline without sand. God's love is impossible to escape, outrun, or outdo. It is everywhere.

Singleness is layered with nuances. Not all who are single have the same perspectives, beliefs, or desires. You may be actively dating right now, in pursuit of a spouse. You may have decided not to date and instead focus your time and energy on another area of your life. You may be seeking God for wisdom in what the best path might be for you. Know that in all of it, you are loved. As you seek a relationship, seek contentment, or seek direction, you do not have to seek out God's love, for it is present with you now and always.

In His love, God gave up everything for you with no guarantee of reciprocity. In love, He emptied Himself on the cross and was obedient unto death. And as if Calvary was not enough, the persistent love of God expands millenia and meets you here today in your singleness. God's love continues to give as it blesses you with every spiritual blessing in the heavens (Ephesians 1:3).

Jesus did not hold back His love for you and never will. Humbling Himself, He became a servant, that He, through His love, might win you back to God. His love gave it all for you. God has loved the world in a way that caused Him to send His only Son to save us (John 3:16). Human love fails at every attempt to amount to a love like this, worthy of our worship. Our selfish efforts crumble to ashes in comparison to the atoning love of God. His love is sacrificial. It will not change if you find a spouse. It will remain even if you never marry. It is constant in the unknown.

The love of God may sound like just another Christian cliché. But perhaps the best clichés exist because they have proven themselves to be true. And yes, it is true—you can stake your life on God's love for you. You can bet on it every time. You can let it be the foundation of your being and doing. His love is so determined and strong that you could never escape it. It is love that is all-consuming and ever-present. His love for you is great—the most enduring, most pure form of affection you have ever or will ever know. His love is indestructible and imperishable. It will not move. Regardless of who does or does not pursue you, God's love always will.

Though you may feel as though your life sometimes lacks the love you want, you will always have the love you need in your heavenly Father.

When your greatest fear has come true before your very eyes, when you think you have messed up too badly this time, when your friends turn away from you, even if your father and mother forsake you, when your joy is overflowing, when all your prayers are answered, when your mouth is full of laughter—God's love remains with you in your loneliness and cheers you on in your contentment. It will shroud you like the plushest of blankets, enveloping every hurt, hesitation, and musing. It will animate your joy.

Many things in this life depend on the decisions you make, the talent you have, or the amount you can afford. God's love is not one of them. You are loved by your Creator and Savior.

God's love is *impossible to escape, outrun,* or *outdo.* It is *everywhere.*

Regardless of who does
or does not pursue you,
God's love always will.

Reflection

How can you trust God when you are lonely?

How does it encourage you to know that you will always have the love you need in Christ?

There is no hierarchy of needs with Jesus.
He cares about you. He cares about
the things you care about.

From Disgraced to Daughter

MARK 5:22–34

At times, we may be tempted to believe that others' needs are more pressing and more important than our own. Our needs may seem selfish when they are all we are responsible for. The troubles that others face may be more apparent. They may have weightier implications. Their needs may affect many people while ours affect only us. When we look around us, we see people who struggle financially. Others battle mental illness. Some are dying.

In comparison, our issues seem small and trivial. We may even have friends and family who tell us so. We may have learned early on to keep our concerns to ourselves—to not overreact or seem too needy. We would not dare open our mouths to ask for help, knowing that someone else may need the help more than we do. We hide in shame, thinking no one will ever stop to care about or understand our plight. We wonder to ourselves, *Does Jesus really care how singleness affects me? Does it matter enough for Him to listen?*

Mark 5 teaches us that Jesus does care about what we feel and experience. His time is not limited as He tends to us and lifts any shame we might feel from our singleness.

When we look to Scripture, we see the Lord display care for His children. Even while on His way to heal someone else, Jesus stopped to minister to a woman who had been suffering for twelve years. Many doctors had failed her, but she had heard of His miracles and power to heal. She was regarded as unclean—day after day, year after year—and knew that He was her only hope. She knew that if she could just reach out and touch Him, she would be healed. As masses of people pressed against Him, she extended her hand and reached for the hem of His garment. Though much was at stake for this woman, she knew that reaching for Jesus was worth the risk.

This woman risked public humiliation and the potential for rejection, but in an instant, she sensed healing in her body, and Jesus felt power go out from Himself. Jesus was on His way to heal Jairus's dying daughter, but first, He asked who touched Him. He wanted the woman to reveal herself. Hemorrhaging no longer, the woman showed herself to Jesus. "'Daughter,' he said to her, 'your faith has saved you. Go in peace and be healed from your affliction'" (Mark 5:34).

Jesus stopped and took the time to attend to this woman's needs. He did not scold her for bothering Him though He was on His way to help someone else. He did not tell her that He was too busy. And in these moments, what once brought her disgrace became only a memory.

Jesus has time for you, too. While others might seem to have needs that are more obvious and urgent than your own, He still stops to attend to you. There is no hierarchy of needs with Jesus. He cares about you. He cares about the things you care about. And as He cares for you, He cares for all the needs of the world. Just as He has the power to heal your body, He can heal the assumptions you have about His thoughts toward you. *Does He have any idea how deeply I desire a husband? Is He just going to pass me by and leave me here in this longing?* When you have exhausted all of your resources and there is nowhere else to go, when you cry out to Jesus, He turns around to behold you face-to-face. Dare to reach for Him through the pressing crowd. Think about it: to whom else would you turn?

When you reach for Jesus, He is faithful to respond with tenderness and compassion. He longs to know that you trust Him. Often, the shame of our sin deceives us into believing that He doesn't have time for us or—worse still—that He cannot bear to be in our presence. It might be that your singleness has brought you shame as you wonder if you are undesirable or why you have not been chosen already when it seems that everyone else has been.

We may feel that shame clings to us like dried blood and fear that we are too ashamed to approach Him. But you cannot be too disgraced or unclean for Jesus. When we gaze upon Christ and His compassion for His children, we are reminded that our worth is not found when we escape the woes of singleness—it is found in Him. His touch is what frees us from shame.

While a touch from Him dried up an unceasing flow of blood in the woman we read about, the blood that flowed from Calvary cleansed us from all our iniquity. Though our sin was like scarlet, He made us white as snow (Isaiah 1:18). And if Jesus did not turn away from you in your sin, He will certainly then not turn away from you in your singleness.

When Jesus is the only hope you have, you are right where you need to be. He desires to redeem you. And when you fear that Jesus is on His way to everyone's house but your own—the one where you dwell in your singleness—He pauses to pursue you. Where you feel others may label your singleness a disgrace, Jesus calls you *daughter.*

When Jesus is the only hope you have, *you are right where you need to be.*

Reflection

How does Jesus free us from the shame we might feel being single?

In your singleness, how does it encourage you to know that Jesus has time for you?

We wear a new reality, for we are defined
not by our singleness but *by our sonship in Christ.*

Adopted as Sons

GALATIANS 3:26–4:7

Picture the scene. The phone lights up, and the adoption agency's number flashes across the screen. It is the call this couple has been waiting for—the one they began to think they may never receive. After years of waiting and praying, they will finally welcome a child into their home. They know that everything will change. They will have to adjust their finances, their furniture, and their sleep.

Even so, they anticipate, with great joy, receiving their baby son into their care. They will give him the family name and dress him in new clothes. They will raise him as their own and grant to him all the resources that belong to them. One day when they have become gray and gone on, everything they have will belong to him. After all, he is their son.

Sometimes, singleness leaves us wondering how to relate to God. We hear much about His heart for marriage and His heart for families. But how does God relate to us when we don't have those things? Who are we to Him as individuals? When we accept Christ, God, too, adopts us as His children (Galatians 4:5)—He is our heavenly Father. We wear a new reality, for we are defined not by our singleness but by our sonship in Christ.

In fact, God's family members are not defined by any of the categories of culture. God's family members are not defined by their economic or familial status. The rich, the poor, and the in-between are welcomed into the dynasty of God through faith in His Son, Jesus Christ. Because of Christ, slave and free, Jew and Greek, male and female, married and single are all considered not just children—but sons.

What Paul's original audience would have understood is that sons received more inheritance, more honor, and more status than daughters. Yes, in Christ, even daughters are sons—not physical sons but sons through spiritual adoption into the eternal kingdom of God. We receive all the inheritance of an heir (Romans 8:17).

While nothing changes about our anatomy or appearance, everything changes about the posture of God toward us. We receive all the rights and privileges of the Son He loves, having uninhibited access to the throne room of our heavenly Father. In Him, we are heirs along with Christ, receiving from God the same spirit that intimately calls out, "*Abba*, Father." At Jesus's baptism, God declared from the heavens, "This is my beloved Son, with whom I am well-pleased" (Matthew 3:17). Through Jesus, God the Father makes the same declaration over us. He delights in His children.

Just as we are no longer separated from God, we are no longer separated from one another. Christ unites us to God and to fellow believers. Thus, the family of

God is created. Those who call on the name of Jesus are adopted as sons and are children of God—brothers and sisters through faith. Wherever you may find yourself on the globe, you can find your family, as God's kinship is not bound by nation or tribe.

What is your definition of family? Are you longing for someone to belong to? Are you longing for people who belong to you? The family of God is the truest and largest family on earth. No longer are we wandering strangers trying to make it through. We have somewhere to belong. We have Someone to belong to. We belong to God—we belong to a kingdom bigger than ourselves.

We are adopted and included and endowed with all the riches of heaven that have come to be ours by the blood of Jesus. When we cry out, "*Abba*, Father," we express our desire for intimacy that only our heavenly Father can give. He answers us as sons, bringing with Him all the approval and affection that belong to Jesus.

The family of God is the *truest* and largest family on earth. *No longer are we wandering strangers* trying to make it through. *We have somewhere to belong.*

We belong to God—

we belong to a kingdom bigger than ourselves.

Reflection

How is sonship an encouragement in singleness?

How does God's family span time and place and override your singleness?

Like a big brother, *Jesus is able to protect us. He saves us from the lies that threaten us* and from the accuser who seeks to smear our name.

Christ Our Brother

HEBREWS 2:11, ROMANS 8:29

To a newly promoted freshman student, the large building filled with intimidating upperclassmen can be overwhelming. Some of us may have to reach further back in our memories to retrieve the sight, but if we try hard enough, we may be able to remember the feeling. *Who will we sit with at lunch? What if people are mean?* In fact, some of us may have experienced the relentless taunting of a bully. Our clothes may not have been cool enough. Our bodies may have been considered too small or too big. Rumors and false accusations may have circulated the staircases and mercilessly shredded our good names. Some of us remember and shudder.

Like a freshman on the first day of high school, we can be intimidated by the vastness of our reality. We are filled with dread as we face life's hallways alone. As single women, we long for someone to stand down our enemies. We want someone to help us out. If only there had been someone bigger, someone stronger, someone more powerful and well-respected to step in and protect us.

What would have been different about those harrowing high school years if we would have had someone like an older brother, who had walked those halls before? No one would dare come against him. He would look out for you with diligence and determination. His heart would be for you, to make sure that you could get to your classes and get your locker open. He would love you so dearly that he would put his reputation on the line just to associate with you.

In the unknown, the known, and the utterly terrifying, in wondering if we will be alone forever, in wondering who will take care of us when we are older, Christ is our true big brother (Hebrews 2:11). Jesus has seen everything we have seen and even what we have never seen before. He has faced everything we face. He has heard it all before. He has beheld the back alleys of this life and knows them in and out. It matters that He is our brother. He has not only faced the inevitable woes of being human, but He has overcome them. Like a big brother, He is able to protect us. He saves us from the lies that threaten us and from the accuser who seeks to smear our name. We are defended. We are helped. Nothing reaches us without first going through Him.

Not only does He know the ins and outs of this life, but Jesus also knows the heart of the Father intimately and fully. For this reason, He is able to assist us. He aided us first in His living, dying, and rising. He aids us now as He stands before the throne of God as our Advocate. He helps us by making us more like Himself. He conforms us into an image that is just like His—obedient and pleasing to the Father.

Are you needy? Are you rejected? Do you feel forsaken? Are you afraid that it will always be like this? Sometimes being single feels like being defenseless. At times, it seems like no one is there to take up for us or to help us do the heavy lifting of life. Fear not, little sister. Your big brother is in the room. He saves, and He protects. Life is liveable because we know Him. Life is joyous because we are known by Him.

Nothing reaches us without first going through Him.

Fear not, little sister.
Your big brother is in the room.
He saves, and He protects.

Reflection

In what areas do you feel vulnerable as a single person?

How does Jesus's protection fill you with peace in your singleness?

When age, distance, and singleness isolate us from time with biological family, *we have family in Christ.*

Brothers and Sisters in Christ

EPHESIANS 4:1–2, 1 PETER 2:17

A certain camaraderie typically exists among siblings, whether spoken or unspoken. The older siblings watch out for the younger ones. They protect them and teach them. Younger siblings look up to the older ones, wanting to imitate them. They admire them and their maturity.

Siblings share a lot of things. They often share the physical features of their parents. They share their belongings and their food. Siblings may also disagree—often. They do not always see eye to eye. Yet, for their family's sake, they forge through and learn to get along. Many times, the older that siblings become, the closer they become. Brothers and sisters often grow close as friends as they age, sharing the memories of the years they have experienced together. Siblings not only share kin, but they also share a unique bond.

Those who belong to the Father are His children. Naturally, His children become siblings in the One who gave His life to unite them and all things together. When age, distance, and singleness isolate us from time with biological family, we have family in Christ. We can find family in the church. This can be tricky—perhaps even trickier than it is for natural siblings. We now bear responsibility for one another.

We have a unique command to love one another and to show honor to each other (Ephesians 4:2, 1 Peter 2:17). God's children come from all different kinds of backgrounds. They have diverse experiences and perceptions. They do not always view life and its affairs the same way. Yet, God calls them to unity. His desire is that they keep the bond of peace and that they show patience because of the love that they share in Christ.

This bond of peace and showing of patience are not easy, especially when the way that you experience life as a single woman is different from how many of your brothers and sisters in Christ experience it. You may be tempted to give up on finding fellowship in the church. You might want to remove yourself from your local church altogether. After all, what is the point of showing up to a place where you are continually misrepresented and misunderstood? Many have asked this question.

You may have wondered if staying is worth it. But what if enduring the discomfort or hardship allows you to get to the other end of the strife? It is possible to live out what God intended for us. Pursuing unity in the church is not something God asks us to do arbitrarily. He longs to give us a family—one that understands us, one that shares a common faith and a common love. What if instead of retreating from the difficulties of being patient and loving, we embraced them and dared to let our brothers and sisters see the innermost places of our hearts? There, they would grow in their empathy and you would grow in yours.

Living at peace as brothers and sisters will not always be easy, but it will be better than you could imagine. God has planned beautiful and rich relationships for you somewhere within His family. Though you do not have a husband right now, you do have brothers and sisters with a common Father. They are there for you to call on, lean on, worship with, eat with, and laugh with. This is a gift from God.

If you want to experience belonging and kinship—kinship not just found in a husband—look no further than the built-in community of God's children. Dare to let yourself be known by them. And in turn, be a place where they can be known. It is worth the tension. They are worth the struggle.

> *He longs to give us a family—*
> one that understands us,
> one that shares a common
> faith and a common love.

Living at peace as brothers and sisters will not always be easy, but it *will be better than you could imagine.*

Reflection

In what ways can you let yourself be known by others in your singleness?

As a single person in your church, how can you be a safe place for others to be known?

This is what makes the good news so good—
that *everyone can now be included*
in the household of God!

Members of God's Household

EPHESIANS 2:11–22

Have you ever felt excluded? Perhaps you have felt left out by a friend group or a team or from a conversation on a subject you know nothing about. Maybe you have felt unseen by a store that sells only at certain price points or sizes.

At times, we may feel like our singleness keeps us isolated. Something about being married and having a family of our own looks more inclusive than being unmarried. On a much deeper level, the Gentiles of the Apostle Paul's day could relate. To be a Gentile simply means to not be Jewish. On the surface, that may not sound like a big deal. But the Jewish people were God's chosen ones. Jesus Himself, the Messiah, descended from them.

So, it was no wonder that there was some friction between Jews and

Gentiles in the churches of Ephesus, the believers to whom Paul addressed his letter. The Gentiles knew nothing of the traditions of the Jewish people. They had no idea of the covenants, the festivals, or even the prophecies about the coming Messiah. How could they possibly be included in such a longstanding legacy?

But nothing excludes any of us—even in singleness—from the family of God if we have placed our faith in Jesus. To the previously excluded, Paul preached the good news. To the Jews who were already included, the plan of God was revealed. Those who were foreigners are now kin. Those who were strangers are now citizens (Ephesians 2:13). This is what makes the good news so good—that everyone can now be included in the household of God!

God has made Jew and Gentile one through Jesus. He made peace between two groups, destroying the hostility between them. He went beyond just making them civil with one another—He made them family. And though Gentiles were not originally privy to the traditions of Israel, God was still pleased to add them to the foundation of the apostles and prophets. God has also brought you near. Regardless of what it looks like, you are included in His plan.

Something much bigger than us is happening here—His plan is greater than what we could imagine. We are participants in a miracle! God's global family is a miraculous act of divine intervention. Those who did not know God can now know Him intimately. We can all be brought near, for God rests His very presence here with Jew and Gentile alike as they look to Christ for salvation. Jesus gave His life for all to be a part of this building. We all have the same access to God through Jesus by His Spirit. Not by tradition or the work of the flesh does anyone enter in—but by the will of God (John 1:13). God does not want you to spectate from the outside. Do not let a bare ring finger keep you from enjoying life in God's household.

Also important to remember—not only has God brought together Jew and Gentile, He has ransomed all kinds of people to Himself. Regardless of whether someone is married, widowed, or a single parent, whether someone is twenty-five or ninety-five, that person can have a place in the household of God. Do not ever forget it; do not take it for granted.

It can be easy to feel excluded when you do not have a spouse to share your life with, when you find yourself surrounded by seemingly happy couples. But with the blood of His only Son, God purchased your place in His family.

Do not miss the blessing of belonging. Lift up your eyes. Look what God has done! You have a place in this house—even when you may feel your singleness excludes you—you have a place. Christ went to great lengths to secure your spot in this holy dwelling.

As a single woman, you too belong here. In your waiting, in your questioning, in your longing—you belong.

You belong here.

> God's global family is a *miraculous act of divine intervention.*

Do not let a bare ring finger keep you from *enjoying life in God's household.*

Reflection

In addition to singleness, are there any other aspects of your life that have made you feel excluded?

In your loneliness, how does Jesus bring you near?

Are you willing to *hold your time, money, and talent with open hands, ready to give,* so that no one in your church community has any lack?

The Perfect Family

ACTS 2:42–47

What if your church was perfect? What if every time you walked in the door, everyone knew your name and asked about the prayer requests you shared? What if you received multiple invitations to join your brothers and sisters and their children for lunch after church? What if they were interested in your life and in your story? What if your singleness did not inhibit your sense of belonging in your community of faith? What if you never had a need—at least that your church family knew of—because they made sure to meet any need you had?

For some of us, this is our beautiful reality. For others, this is just a dream. Whatever your situation, the early church in Acts gives us a glimpse of what a familial biblical community is supposed to look like—people united under the name of Jesus in love, devotion, and care.

The book of Acts shows us the family of God at its best, thriving in community with one another. Fresh from the winds of Pentecost, where the Holy Spirit descended in the upper room (Acts 2:1–2), followers of Jesus gathered together to share their lives with one another. They ate meals together. They were generous with their possessions. They made sure no one among them lacked anything they needed (Acts 2:44).

The believers in the early church were united around the testimony of Jesus. They believed so much in Jesus—His life, death, and resurrection from the dead—that they devoted their lives not just to Him but to each other.

Is the family of God something that you are willing to devote your life to? Are you willing to hold your time, money, and talent with open hands, ready to give, so that no one in your church community has any lack?

Of course, this is a group effort. You should not be the only one in your church family making these types of sacrifices. It can be difficult to know how to respond when your church community is not one to make sure everyone is included and taken care of. If this is something you feel is missing in your church, then begin to pray!

Pray that God would make the community of believers you belong to radically devoted to each other. Pray that the Holy Spirit would work so powerfully in the hearts of your church that you all cannot help but be generous, thoughtful, and inviting to people in all different seasons of life—whether single, married, widowed, divorced, dating, or engaged—to everyone.

In your singleness, you may sometimes feel distant from the life of your church. It seems as if families only interact with other families. Sometimes it can be hard to see where you belong. But you do belong, even when those around you have not yet caught the vision. What we do not see in this passage is anyone being left out because of their marital status—or anything else for that matter.

The truth is, there is no perfect family. Not even God's family is perfect—not yet anyway. One day, when we are in heaven with Jesus, we will be the perfect family. But until then, we strive toward this kind of unabashed community. It will take much patience and bearing with one another in love to accomplish God's ideal for us. And though it is not a fast or easy process to learn to live as an intimate family community, may we make it our aim.

Pray that God would make the community of believers you belong to *radically devoted to each other.*

One day, when we are
in heaven with Jesus,
we will be the perfect family.

Reflection

How have you experienced your church family care for you in your singleness?

Write a short prayer to God asking Him to help you and others who are single become united, seen, and known in your church.

The love of God is something that
we as believers are meant to understand
together, *in community with one another.*

Understanding Together

EPHESIANS 3:14–21

"Teamwork makes the dream work!"

This is a phrase you have likely heard before. Many activities we participate in require working closely with others. Whether it be a group project, a work presentation, or tag-teaming chores with a roommate, some things we just cannot do alone, and Paul seeks to communicate this in Ephesians 3. He explains that now that God has made all of them one through Jesus, they can now work together to go even deeper in their relationship with Him.

Being faithful followers of Jesus was something that the Ephesians would not be able to do without one another. The Apostle Paul explains that God's love is expansive and immeasurable. It is something that they need God's power to understand. And not only do they need spiritual power, but they need the help of their brothers and sisters in the faith. So, too, do we. The truth is, we are not meant to live the Christian life on our own.

This does not mean that you are not meant to be single but that you are meant to live in community with other believers.

You need your brothers and sisters in Christ. The love of God is something that we as believers are meant to understand together, in community with one another. The task of understanding God's love is so grand that we need help (Ephesians 3:18), and this has always been God's plan. The body of Christ needs you—and you do not have to be married to give or receive this help.

Not only do you need other believers in your life reflecting the love of God to you, but you are also meant to be a reflection as well. God created you to be a mirror of His love—shown through Christ's sacrifice on the cross—through the way that you show love to others. You were made to testify to others about the goodness of God in your life and throughout all of history. We all need each other to point out just how good He is—in seasons of feeling lonely, in seasons of waiting, and in the seasons of joy that come as well.

Being a part of God's family is one big group project—one that we will never complete in this life. Until we get to heaven, we only partially see the height, depth, width, and length of God's love. But while we wait for that day, there is work to do in our church communities. God wants to fill all of us with all of His fullness. With all the saints, by the power of the Holy Spirit, we can know Him more deeply than we can on our own as we remind each other of His goodness.

You do not need anything more than you have now to be an asset to the family of God. You do not have to have a boyfriend or be engaged or have a husband to have value here. There is not a status you must reach. Right now—in whatever circumstance you find yourself, in whatever season of life, you are needed here.

It will require diligence. It will take intentionality, and it will take trust in the Lord. But you have the opportunity to experience God's love together with the body of Christ. This is a beautiful invitation that God extends to all of His children — none are excluded. What a privilege it is to know His love. What an opportunity we have to know Him and grow in understanding of Him together!

> *We all need each other to point out just how good He is —*
> in seasons of feeling lonely,
> in seasons of waiting, and in the
> seasons of joy that come as well.

You do not need anything more than you have now to be an asset to the family of God.

You do not have to have a boyfriend or be engaged or have a husband to have value here.

Reflection

Why might single believers need other Christians to help them understand God's love?

How can single believers help married Christians understand God's love?

Be an active participant in
the unity Christ bought for us.

Above All, Through All, In All

EPHESIANS 4:1–6, ACTS 6:1–7

The thread of unity runs throughout the book of Ephesians. Christians are meant to be one. Because we are human, however, we do not always get this right—it can still be a struggle to live into the truth of our unity as Christ followers. Sometimes in the Church, it can feel like there are all kinds of divisions. For single people, the needs of married people—particularly families—may often seem to eclipse the needs of single people. This is not an intentional omission, but it can be hurtful all the same.

Sadly, in our singleness, this omission can cause us to feel separated and divided from our brothers and sisters in Christ—but this should never be. While not all churches are this way, this is an experience common to many singles. Yet, God is determined that we be one.

We will certainly never get unity right every time; however, we must remember that the bond we have as Christians is much stronger than the things that divide us (Ephesians 4:4–6). But how can we be unified when we feel so unseen? What do we do when the very entity we are created to be a part of seems to forget our needs as singles?

For answers to these questions, we can look to Scripture for guidance. A group of widows in the book of Acts were being overlooked (Acts 6:1). In the daily distribution of food, they were not receiving what they needed. When this was brought to the attention of the apostles, they appointed seven men to oversee the distribution, securing fair treatment for the widows who had slipped under the radar. The widows needed an advocate, but they had to first advocate for themselves. Though we would often prefer to have our needs met without having to articulate them, this expectation is not always realistic.

You may have to bring your needs to the attention of someone who can do something about it. Talk to a pastor or leader about your needs and the needs of other people like you in your church. Ask how you can foster an environment of unity in the church where you worship. Find other believers who are in a similar place in life and figure out how you can be a blessing to your congregation. Talk to older single people in your congregation and ask them how they connect with other believers who have different family dynamics. Be an active participant in the unity Christ bought for us.

Though we might not be united to a husband in marriage, we are united in the family of God by one Lord—Jesus, who loved us and died for us. We are united by one faith—our corporate belief that Jesus is exactly who He says He is. We are united by one baptism—the sign of the covenant of grace that Christ made with us all. We all have one heavenly Father who permeates all things. He is the One we are to spend our days glorifying.

No one said it would be easy. In fact, Paul wrote a long letter to the churches in Ephesus to explain what unity in the body should look like. And though we strive to get it right, we will still stumble, trip, and become frustrated with one another, but that's what family does. The body of Christ is not an entity made up of individual families. Rather, it is a global family made up of individuals who have made a decision to follow Jesus. The bond we have in Jesus is more powerful than anything that might try to tear us apart.

> *We are united by one faith—* our corporate belief that *Jesus is exactly who He says He is.*

The bond we have in Jesus is *more powerful* than anything that might try to tear us apart.

Reflection

How is our bond as believers stronger than the things that try to divide us?

How can you humbly bring your needs as a single person to the attention of your church family?

One of the sweetest things about this family of God is that *every woman can be a mother and every man can be a father, whether or not their children bear their surname.*

Spiritual Mothers

TITUS 2:3–5

One of the hardest things for some singles, particularly women, is the desire for motherhood. Being unmarried, there is little way of knowing if motherhood can ever be a reality. Of course, many married women experience the heartache of infertility and its devastating emotional and mental consequences. The single woman experiences an ache as well when she is left wondering not only if her womb will ever be filled with little ones who look like her, but also whether or not she will ever be married. Her dream of a family of her own hangs heavily in her heart, like a question mark at the end of a sentence.

Having the desire, ability, and need to nurture with no outlet is a peculiar phenomenon. If this is you, you are not alone. Know that God sees and understands. Many women like you are in this global family God has created.

One of the sweetest things about this family of God is that every woman can be a mother and every man can be a father, whether or not their children bear their surname. No matter how long you have known Jesus, you still have something to offer the women in your life who have not known Him as long. God allows us to become teachers and nurturers to those in the faith who need mentorship and care.

God has equipped you to raise spiritual children through whatever gifts—encouragement, teaching, hospitality, and more—He has given you. These gifts can be an asset to someone who is coming up after you, yearning to know the ways of God. In the book of Titus, the Apostle Paul instructed the older women to teach the younger women. We have a responsibility to those who are younger than us.

The blessings of a spiritual mother are innumerable. Where a natural mother may not always be the best role model or example of faith, the spiritual mother has the ability to say, "Imitate me, as I also imitate Christ" (1 Corinthians 11:1). Look around you. Are there any younger women, whether in age or in faith, who you could invest time in? Is there anyone who could use the wisdom you gained from your experiences or the lessons that God has taught you over time?

You can mother right now. The desire, ability, and need to nurture is God-given, useful, and necessary to the body of Christ. The family of God needs your nurturing. The family of God needs your help raising up the next generation of believers to know and love God. It is an honor and a privilege to mother not just in the flesh, but spiritually, too.

Nothing is going to completely fill the desire you have to carry your own children. This longing is difficult to experience and to express to others, especially as a single person. However, know that God is not asking you to forget that dream. He wants you to come to Him with your desires and allow Him to be present with you in the midst of them. In the middle of your wanting, He can give you the ministry of mothering.

Ask Him if there are any practical ways that you, in your singleness, can serve the younger women around you and mother them in the meantime. Use this time of singleness to mother and encourage in ways you may not otherwise have had the opportunity to do. Teach younger women in your life to love and follow Jesus, bringing glory to Him.

> You can mother right now.
> *The desire, ability, and need to nurture is God-given*, useful, and necessary to the body of Christ.

Teach younger women in your life
to love and follow Jesus,
bringing glory to Him.

Reflection

What is the value in being a spiritual mother while you are single?

How might being a spiritual mother help you connect to the family of God?

You were meant to be raised in the faith
by the women God has placed in His body.

Spiritual Daughters

TITUS 2:3–5

Investing in younger women in the faith is a great way to find joy. However, as a member of God's family, you are not just meant to give. You are also meant to receive. Another blessing of spiritual motherhood is the opportunity to be a spiritual daughter (Titus 2:3–5). This is especially true if you live far from your natural family or do not have a close relationship with them. The family of God offers a balm for the ache left by distance, discord, or death. Spiritual mothers, of course, could never replace the bond and proximity you would have with your natural mother. However, receiving the love of a spiritual mother is beautiful and biblical.

Cultivating relationships with and learning from older women in the faith will help you, as a single woman, to experience the benefits of the family of God as you become a spiritual daughter. You were meant to be raised in the faith by the women God has placed in His body. If you do not already have someone that you are spending time learning from, consider asking God to send you a spiritual mother. You have the unique opportunity to learn what it looks like to serve the Lord in singleness—whether you are still waiting for a husband or whether you are perfectly fine without one. Allow another woman into your life to help guide and teach you while you are in this season.

Asking someone to mentor or disciple you in this way can be intimidating—for you and for them. As you build community within your church family, prayerfully, you will begin to build natural relationships with other women. If you are in a small group or Sunday school class that is multigenerational, this could be a great place for you to build friendships with believing women in your circle. If you have someone in mind, ask her to have coffee with you or go to dinner. Often, she would be more than happy to spend time with you.

As the friendship progresses and you both feel comfortable with one another, ask questions about her faith. Ask about her walk with the Lord and how it came to be. We often think of discipleship as something that has to be structured and focused—and that is good! But discipleship can also happen while just living life together and doing the day-to-day—going to the grocery store together, sharing a recipe, or sending a quick text asking for prayer are all opportunities for discipleship.

Make it your prayer that God would provide an older woman in the faith to come alongside you in your pursuit of faithfulness to God. Allow yourself to be mothered by someone who is wiser than you and has walked with the Lord longer than you have. The wisdom of someone who has spent years with Jesus, learning to follow Him and trust Him, is a gift of God's grace to all who encounter her. Be her beneficiary. Learn from her story. Imitate her as she imitates Christ.

Reflection

What is the value in being a spiritual daughter in singleness?

How might being a spiritual daughter help you connect to the family of God?

The Church Needs Aunts

You may have heard some cultures use the nickname "Auntie" to refer to a beloved female family member who may or may not be biologically related. We can learn much from them when it comes to defining family. Regardless of blood kinship, we can play a special role in the lives of the kids around us. We can show up for the ones of whom Jesus said, "let [them] come to me" (Mark 10:14).

Prayerfully, you have begun to make close friends in your local church community with whom you can walk through life. If not, continue to pray that God will send you friends who love Him and who will love you like family. You may even make friends who are married. Some of those married friends may have children you get to spend time with as well. What would it look like for you to play an intentional part in discipling those children in your life?

As Christians, we are all called to be disciple-makers, intentionally teaching others how to follow Jesus. As the family of God, we have a responsibility in the lives of our friends to also be a good witness for their children.

When you are blessed with deeply formed friendships that have come from a shared faith in Jesus, you are experiencing the benefits of the family of God. Your friends are now your brothers and sisters in Christ. What is even sweeter is that you can be an aunt to their kids. You can help them disciple their children. You can point their children to Jesus. You can repeat and reinforce what their children hear from them and what they hear in church. The family of God is a true village in which we are responsible for one another. We can love our sisters and brothers in Christ by loving their children well.

Taking on the role of an aunt is not a small thing. Talk with your friends about how you can play a role in their kids' lives. The definition of family grows and expands in God's kingdom as do our own roles and responsibilities. The Church needs aunts to help point its youngest participants to Jesus.

Your singleness is not wasted—ever. There is a purpose for you in the family of God. As you grow in your faith and love for Jesus, consider the little ones around you. Your life can be an example for them. You might be waiting to be married and have children of your own—or maybe you don't plan to have kids of your own at all. Either way, in the love you have for your brothers and sisters in Christ, love their kids, too.

> Regardless of blood kinship, *we can play a special role in the lives of the kids around us.*

In whatever season of life we may find ourselves in — *even in singleness* — our Father is there with us.

Indispensable

1 CORINTHIANS 12:12–31

The smallest organ in your body is the pineal gland. This tiny mass in your brain is responsible for regulating your circadian sleep rhythms by receiving light cues from the retina. During dark hours, your pineal gland releases melatonin, causing your body to get quality sleep. Though small, the pineal gland plays an important role in the functions of your body. After all, we know that our bodies need sleep. The pineal gland helps us get it. How peculiar that the tiniest organ has such a big job to do.

Just as your pineal gland, small as it is, has an important function in your body, you have an important function in the body of Christ. Your role might be more prominent, like a position of leadership. Your role might be behind the scenes as a greeter or in production. However "big" or "small," it matters. Wherever you find yourself serving in your local church, know that your role is important. Know that *you* are important—not because of what you can do, but because of who God is.

The Apostle Paul addresses these very thoughts when he says, "And if the ear should say, 'Because I'm not an eye, I don't belong to the body,' it is not for that reason any less a part of the body" (1 Corinthians 12:16). In the same way, we cannot say, "Because I am single, I don't belong to the body." Marriage is not a qualifier for kingdom belonging and service. The body of Christ needs single people just as much as it needs married people. It takes all of us to reflect the love and goodness of Jesus to one another and to the watching world.

God, who needs nothing from any of us, allows us all to be a part of His work in the church and in the world. It is His desire that you take your place here. You—even with a bare ring finger. Marriage does not and will not make you any more important to the function of the body than you already are, just as singleness does not make you any less important.

As a single person, you may have questioned how you could ever be an asset to your church or to the body of Christ as a whole. You might doubt your significance in the church or think that the role you play is smaller than someone who is married with a family of their own. Maybe the lifestyles of the leaders you see are much different than your own. You might question your place and your value.

Being single can make you feel isolated sometimes. It can be hard to see just how you fit. *But you do fit.* And being a part of the functions of your local church will help you build community and a stronger sense of what is already true—that you belong to the family of God.

Reflection

In what ways can you use your spiritual gifts to serve the family of God while you are single?

Why are single people needed to equip the church?

When you are overwhelmed by all of the
responsibilities you must carry on your own,
*look to your Savior. Jesus knows
what it is like to do it all alone.*

Our Single Savior

JOHN 1, 1 PETER 5:7

Are you tired of doing everything alone? You just got home from work, and the trash is overflowing . . . again. You haven't checked the mail in days. Your car needs an oil change. A warning notice is on the door from the city saying that the grass is overgrown. The entire house needs to be cleaned. The refrigerator is empty, signaling that it is time for another trip to the grocery store. The water bill needs to be paid, and it can only be paid in person. Meanwhile, the rest of the bills need to be paid, too — rent, electricity, internet, medical bills, car payment. Finally, on top of that, your paycheck is the only money there is. Your job alone has to pay for everything. As you run the numbers for the umpteenth time, you wonder how you have even made it this far.

It is okay to feel the way you feel. The burden of singleness can be heavy in many ways. Not only are you lacking the romance that you desire, but you may be lacking help and additional income. If you are overwhelmed, know that you do not need to feel ashamed. You do not need to feel guilty if you find that even daily, mundane tasks are difficult to do all by yourself. When you are overwhelmed by all of the responsibilities you must carry on your own, look to your Savior. Jesus knows what it is like to do it all alone. He is with you, and He will give you the strength you need. Jesus is enough as He walks with you through your singleness.

Jesus is the One through whom all things have been created (John 1:10). He alone took on flesh and dwelled among us (John 1:14). Jesus, by Himself, entered a world full of demands and responsibilities. He was a son, a friend, and a teacher. Not only this, but He is God. While He met the physical and emotional needs of those around Him, He was also about to take on the greatest rescue plan in history to save all of humanity from the penalty of sin. All by Himself.

Jesus, by Himself, did everything required to save you. Alone, He wept in Gethsemane. Alone He went to the cross. Alone He died the death of a criminal. Alone He was buried in a borrowed tomb. Alone He rose again from the grave. Alone He ascended into heaven where He sits now—at the Father's side, interceding for you. Jesus alone inaugurated a new family to which the children of God belong.

Because Jesus is enough, you are enough. Just as you are. In the season you are in. Even though you have no spouse to speak of. No, you are not Jesus. You cannot do everything by yourself, and sometimes you will have no choice but to reach out to your spiritual family and ask for help. You might spend a lot of time before God asking Him for the strength to do everything that is set before you to do each day. But Jesus—in Himself—is enough to give you the strength you need.

When the bills are due and it is time to go to the store again, when the laundry pile topples over and you want to crumble too, when no one else is responsible but you and you feel your shoulders are not broad enough to carry the weight of the world, remember Jesus. His life, death, and resurrection are enough to satisfy. When it is all up to you, you can leave it all up to Him (1 Peter 5:7). When you are alone, Jesus alone is enough.

Because Jesus is enough,
you are enough. Just as you are.

When no one else is responsible but you and you feel your shoulders are not broad enough to carry the weight of the world, *remember Jesus.*

Reflection

How does it encourage you to know that Jesus lived His entire life as a single person?

In what ways is Jesus enough for you in your singleness?

A Poem of Praise to Our Single Savior

All-sufficient Savior
It was enough

Your life

Alone

Your perfect obedience
Enough
To satisfy

Jesus
It was enough

Your death

Alone

The work You finished
Enough
To satisfy

All-sufficient Savior
You are enough

Your presence

Alone

When I am alone
Enough
To satisfy

Jesus
You are enough

Your glory

Alone

Is
Enough
To satisfy

You have a family that extends beyond
the one given to you by birth.
You belong to the global family of God.

True Family

MARK 3:34–35

Distance in family relationships can complicate singleness. As you grow older, family relationships begin to change. You move out of your parents' home. Your siblings likely have their own lives and maybe their own families. Maybe God has called you to a place far away from your family. Or maybe there is distance from your natural family because they do not love the Lord or love you the way they should. Strain in family relationships can make singleness harder and more lonely.

Whatever the reason might be for distance in your familial relationships, your singleness might make it feel even less bearable. While it is okay to grieve the closeness you wish you had with your family, whether in proximity or emotional connection, you can be encouraged. You have a family that extends beyond the one given to you by birth. You belong to the global family of God.

Jesus was misunderstood and isolated from His biological family. In fact, they thought He was out of His mind for the way He was carrying out His ministry (Mark 3:21). They were too caught up in worldly concerns to see how God was working His will through His Son. For this reason, Jesus said that His *true* family is composed of those who know the will of His Father and do it (Mark 3:34–35).

Though your family might be distant, your ring finger bare, and your home absent of the laughter of your own children, you do have a family. You, who have trusted in the will of God and have placed your faith in Jesus, are in the true family of God. Jesus's true family is now your true family.

Jesus loved His earthly family. But He recognized that the bond enjoyed by those who love God is stronger and more true than the bond He had with His earthly family. The family of God is the purest and most true—and it is eternal.

No, your Christian family is not yet a perfect family. But the family of Jesus is the family that agrees about who Jesus is—the Christ, the Son of God, the Savior of the world. The family of God is truer than the closest of natural relatives.

Our natural families are a good gift from God. But they may not always understand your love for God, and they may not always be near. The familial bonds of the family of God are held together by Jesus Himself, who gave it all to redeem us from sin and bind believers together.

If you are both single and distanced from your family, remember that Jesus has welcomed you into His. Be encouraged by the fact that you are not the only one who feels this way. Lean into the relationships you have with other Christians, knowing that they, too, are your true family.

Reflection

How does being a part of Jesus's family help us when we are single and feel distant from our biological family?

In your singleness, what are the benefits of having a family who agrees on who Jesus is?

A Liturgy for Taking Out the Trash

You once knelt down in the dirt
Writing with Your hands
Granting dignity to the disgraced
If You could do that
I can
Do this one thing
Once a week or twice
Remembering that You
Choose what is lowly
Even me
And You
Make all miseries
Mercy
Even this

You once washed feet
Cleansing with care
Those You loved
If You could do that
I can
Do this one thing
Once a week or twice
Remembering that You
Make all things clean
Even me

And You
Make all grime
Grace
Even this

You once were covered in blood
Stained with spit
Atoning for my sin
If You could do that
I can
Do this one thing
Once a week or twice
Remembering that You
Chose the mess
Just for me
And You
Make all suffering
Sacred
Even this

Amen.

Your life and its outcome *do not revolve around* whether or not you are married.

Anna the Widowed Prophetess

LUKE 2:36–38

Often, singleness involves a great deal of pondering the future. We wonder how long we will be single. We wonder how we are going to adjust to our actual lives rather than the lives we thought we would have had by now. We wonder if we will always be alone. And, if we do end up single for the rest of our lives, *How will we survive? What will we do with the hurt and disappointment that accompany broken dreams? What will our lives look like down the road?*

These are all valid questions and concerns. However, we need to understand an important truth about singleness and how it relates to the rest of our lives: your purpose in life is bigger than your singleness. Your life and its outcome do not revolve around whether or not you are married. If you end up single for the rest of your life, you can yet live a life that is blessed and full of God's grace.

In Scripture we see a compact cameo of a woman named Anna (Luke 2:36–38). From this brief narrative, we learn that Anna was married to her husband for seven years before he died. After those seven years, she spent her life as a widow for the next eighty-four years. Anna spent those eighty-four years worshiping the Lord in the temple. Day in and day out, she fasted, prayed, and praised God.

On a day just like any other day, Mary and Joseph came into the temple with the Christ child in their arms. Anna, a prophetess, knew immediately that she was looking into the face of the hope of all the world. She and other faithful worshipers in Jerusalem had been waiting for Jesus's arrival all their lives. Upon seeing Him, Anna began to worship and testify about the arrival of the Savior to all who had put their hope and faith in the coming Messiah.

If we add up the years that Anna was married and the years she was widowed, we can deduce that she was over one hundred years old! Anna's tenure as a wife was just a blip in the timeline of her story. The Bible does not tell us about the emotions and questions that she may have had regarding her widowhood. But what we do know is that her singleness did not keep her from the Lord's purposes. It was in her singleness that her eyes beheld the glory of God. With the gift that God gave her to prophesy, she was able to comfort those who were longing and waiting for the Savior.

Can you open yourself up to what God might have for you in the midst of your singleness? You do not yet know what your eyes will behold in this season. Despite how you may feel, singleness is just a small part of your story. It is just a sentence in the middle of a much longer and more profound story. Like Anna, you can live a life that testifies to the faithfulness and salvation of God. In the family of your heavenly Father, singleness is eclipsed by the grandeur of knowing and belonging to Him.

It is okay to ask questions and wonder what the future might bring. But as you ponder, consider what God might do. If singleness is prolonged or if you never marry, you can live a life of purpose. Yes, you may have to adjust to a reality that is much different from the one you dreamed of. But God is able to give you a life filled with meaning. You can spend the rest of your life telling the story of how God showed you just who He is and how good He has been.

Can you *open yourself up to what God might have for you* in the midst of your singleness?

God is able to give you
a life *filled with meaning.*

Reflection

How was Anna's life significant even though she was only married for a short time?

How does God's goodness help ease the fear of being single for longer than expected?

God does not view our singleness as an obstacle. In fact, when we set our focus on Him and His purposes for us, *He can use our singleness.*

Tabitha the Beloved

ACTS 9:36–42

Do you wonder if you could ever be useful to God's family as a single person? Do your hands feel empty at times—as if not having a spouse means that you do not have a purpose? Sometimes singleness can make us feel like our lives are void of meaning. While deep down we might know it is not true, our thoughts and feelings often tell us lies about our worth.

We falsely equate being single with being less. We associate being alone with being useless. And if we are not careful, we can quickly be given over to hopelessness and despair. We must understand that God does not view our singleness as an obstacle. In fact, when we set our focus on Him and His purposes for us, He can use our singleness.

The book of Acts tells us a story of a disciple named Tabitha. While the Bible does not say whether Tabitha was single or married, we learn important truths from her life. We do not know much about her except that one day she became sick and died. Other disciples who knew Tabitha heard that the Apostle Peter was in a town nearby. Desperate to see her life restored, Tabitha's friends begged Peter to come to the bed where they had laid her. When Peter got there, Tabitha's loved ones, with tears in their eyes, showed him the robes and clothing that she had made for them.

While the Bible never mentions a husband or children, Tabitha clearly meant a lot to the community of believers in which she lived. Not only was she a seamstress who provided them all with the clothing that covered them, but the text also tells us that she was always doing good works. Tabitha's community considered her a vital and valuable member—so much so that they had faith that she could be raised from the dead and restored back to them.

What may sound like just clothes and good deeds meant everything to Tabitha's friends. This is the nature of the family of God. God will use each one of us as a blessing to His people if we let Him. God can multiply into an instrument of favor in the hand of the Lord what may seem like only a small gift or talent in your hands. Serving others through acts that seem like very small deeds in the middle of such an arduous life matter tremendously in the kingdom and family of God. Tabitha's story proves just that. Imagine the joy the disciples felt when Peter presented Tabitha to them alive. For a little while longer, they had her at their side again.

What has the Lord given you to do? What skills or talents do you have that you can use to bless those around you? Do not waste this time thinking about what your life could be like if you were married. Your life right now has value. Your life right now has the potential to bring the goodness of God to bear for you and those in your community.

A lack of marriage is not equal to a lack of meaning. Singleness does not disqualify you from living a significant and worthwhile life. Despite any indication that Tabitha was married, God infused her life with meaning and surrounded her with the love of spiritual family—just as He can do for you.

While you may feel like you wear your singleness like a stain that everyone can see, it is just a blip in your narrative. It does not define you, and it certainly does not disqualify you from living profoundly in the family of God.

As He intended for Tabitha, God intends for your life to be a demonstration of His hand at work—reaching through you to bless His family as a whole. And while you use your gifts, you will be blessed by others who are using theirs. Do not wait to be married to be a servant to someone. Do not wait to be married to be productive. You were meant to belong to something bigger than yourself. You were meant to participate in God's family with just what you have now—just as you are.

Do not waste this time thinking about what your life could be like if you were married. *Your life right now has value.*

Singleness does not disqualify you from living a significant and worthwhile life.

Reflection

How was Tabitha's life full of meaning even though there is no indication in the Bible that she was married?

How does your life bring meaning to your friends and church family?

The gift of celibacy is beautiful
and should be celebrated.

Paul's Gift

MATTHEW 19:11–12,
1 CORINTHIANS 7:7–8

Have you ever received a gift that you thought you would not enjoy? Maybe your aunt gave you a sweater that you would have never picked for yourself. Maybe it even seemed strange at first. Its texture may have been striking. It may have even smelled funny. Yet, once you tried it on, you actually loved it. You were thankful that you had been given a gift that you would not have bought for yourself or experienced otherwise. Maybe now that sweater is hanging in your closet as you anticipate the next cool, crisp fall day.

The Apostle Paul was given a gift, too. Many of us would consider this gift strange, especially in our culture of marriage, family, and children. Sometimes, God gives people the gift of singleness. To some, God has given a special grace to remain single and abstain from sex all of their lives in order to devote themselves to serving Him. This gift is called celibacy.

As we consider our singleness, some of us may sense that God has given us this gift, too. If so, you are in good company. The gift of celibacy is beautiful and should be celebrated. It might just be the gift that God, in His love and kindness, has given you as a blessing you never thought you would enjoy.

From what we can gather from Paul in 1 Corinthians 7:8, he had the gift of singleness. Paul even went so far as to say that he wished everyone had the same gift that he had because it gave him the ability to serve the Lord with a type of freedom that he would not have had if he were married with a family.

While he knew that not all would have the same gift that he had, Paul was grateful for his celibacy. As we see in the books of Acts and throughout the rest of the letters Paul wrote to the church, he traveled a great amount to preach the gospel and to equip churches. God also used Paul to write much of the New Testament. Even though he was single, Paul was an integral part of God's family.

Jesus talked about people such as Paul with the gift of celibacy while He was teaching His disciples about marriage and divorce, saying that this was a gift only some would be able to accept. Jesus likened those who had purposely chosen to forgo marriage and sex for the sake of the kingdom to eunuchs. By "eunuchs," Jesus is referring to men who were celibate, either because they had been castrated or because they had been born without the ability to reproduce (Matthew 19:11–12).

From the Old Testament to the New Testament, we see how the gospel changes the plight of eunuchs. According to the Mosaic law, eunuchs could not participate in public worship, nor could they be included in the priesthood (Deuteronomy 23:1). Yet, what is beautiful about the gospel is that all who place their faith in Jesus now belong to the royal priesthood made up of all of God's children (1 Peter 2:9). We even see Philip preach the gospel to a eunuch from Ethiopia and baptize him (Acts 8:26–40).

Jesus said that this is a gift that only some would be able to accept. And while we may think that celibacy—the gift of remaining unmarried—is just something else that will exclude us, the opposite is true.

You belong here. Though your gift may seem foreign to those who do not understand it, it is good—very good. Like the Apostle Paul, if you have been given the gift of remaining single, you still belong to this heavenly family. God has given you an ability that most do not have. Celibacy—not marriage—will span eternity (Matthew 22:30). You have now what we will receive in heaven. Celebrate this gift. Make the most of it wherever and however God lovingly leads you.

> While we may think that celibacy—the gift of remaining unmarried—is just something else that will exclude us, *the opposite is true.*

Like the Apostle Paul,
if you have been given the gift
of remaining single, *you still
belong to this heavenly family.*

Reflection

In what ways is celibacy a gift?

What does Jesus mean when He says in Matthew 19:12, "The one who is able to accept it should accept it"?

Our imaginations are often not *wild* enough to conceive of any *beauty* that might come from a situation that we do not want and never saw coming.

A Better Redeemer: Ruth's Story

RUTH 3, 4:13–14

Sometimes, when we look at our singleness, we may believe that it is impossible to redeem—we feel like the details are too many and our resources are too few for our stories to have the beautiful ending that we used to dream about. Our imaginations are often not wild enough to conceive of any beauty that might come from a situation that we do not want and never saw coming. Yet, through the story of Ruth, we learn that even through the unexpected events of our lives and difficult outcomes that may sometimes follow, the Lord does not withhold His goodness from those whose faith is founded in Him.

In Ruth's story, an unimaginable and sobering tragedy befell three widows—a mother-in-law and her two sons' brides. After both of their husbands died, the women were left destitute (Ruth 1:1–5). They likely sat bewildered, wondering what could possibly be next. They had no men to provide for them or protect them. They were alone now except for each other.

Naomi decided that she would leave Moab and go back to her homeland of Judah. She urged her daughters-in-law, Ruth and Orpah, to save themselves and go back to their families as well. Orpah heeded the urging, but Ruth refused to leave Naomi. Instead, both women headed to Judah, not knowing what might be ahead.

Upon arriving in Judah, Ruth began to glean in the fields, gathering what she could to provide for herself and Naomi. While doing so, she caught the eye of a man named Boaz, who favored Ruth. He gave orders to his men not to touch her and to let her gather as much grain as she needed (Ruth 2:8–9).

When Naomi heard the name of the man Ruth had encountered, she was excited. The man with whom Ruth had found favor was a kinsman-redeemer in Naomi's family—one who was obligated to marry the widow of a family member who had died (Ruth 2:20), yet there was a redeemer still closer than him (Ruth 3:12). However, when presented with the opportunity to take Ruth as his wife, this redeemer declined (Ruth 4:6). So it was Boaz who took Ruth as his wife. She now had someone to protect and care for her and her mother-in-law (Ruth 4:13).

Before you think that this is some kind of happily-ever-after that does not belong in a book about singleness, think again. Though we see God meet Ruth's faithfulness to Naomi with His faithfulness to them both, that is not all there is to see in this narrative.

This story is not just about Ruth ending up married—this story is actually about Jesus, who would descend from Ruth and Boaz: from their son Obed, to his son Jesse, to his son David—King David—from whose line the Christ would be born (Matthew 1:5).

Jesus is the true and better Boaz. He is the One who has come to redeem us both from sin and from the pit of despair where we might find ourselves. Beloved, we can take the women's words to Naomi in Ruth 4:14 and make them our own today: *Blessed be the Lord, who has not left us without a redeemer!*

Without a husband to speak of—whether you have never been married, whether you have been divorced, or whether you have been widowed—you have been redeemed. You have been purchased at a high price. The blood of Jesus bought you back from the throes of sin and death and placed you into a royal, heavenly family (1 Peter 1:18–19, 1 Peter 2:9). Despite the absence of a wedding ring, you have Someone to care for you.

Like Ruth, you can look back and thank God for the unknown. You can thank Him that, though this was the outcome you never wanted—the one you did not expect—He has not withheld His goodness from you. Like Ruth, you are now included in the family of Jesus. You have been redeemed.

Jesus is the true and better Boaz. He is the One who has come to redeem us both from sin and from the pit of despair where we might find ourselves.

Like Ruth, you are now included
in the family of Jesus.
You have been redeemed.

Reflection

How is Jesus our true and better Kinsman-Redeemer?

How is being redeemed by Jesus a comfort in your singleness?

A Liturgy for Paying the Bills

Upholder of the universe
You sustain my life
Just as sure as You gave me
Breath at my waking this morning
You can give me means to sustain
Light and water
Home and automobile
Tuition and gasoline

Keeper of cattle on a thousand hills
Rich in all things
You give as You will
All my needs are met
In my Father who is
Eternally wealthy
Who can make His means
Flow to me

God of immeasurably more
Whether there is more month than money
And more demand than supply
Or I simply just don't want to
Bear the load alone
Make me grateful
For the conveniences
That make invoices necessary

Master of many mansions
Remind my heart of the One
Who gladly paid the debt I owed
The very same One
Who is providing now for me
Make me wise
Remembering that all my treasures
Are from You and for You

Amen.

When we are weary and frustrated in our singleness, it is important to remember that *we work both for the benefit of our spiritual family and for the glory of God,* knowing that there is blessing in not giving up.

For the Good of All

GALATIANS 6:9–10

It takes years of training to participate in an Olympic event. If you watch the post-race interviews of runners who have just completed a race, they will often talk about all of the work it took to lead them to where they are now. They put in strenuous exercise over countless hours for months and years at a time. Then, they have to run the actual race. There is no doubt that they get tired sometimes. There are not many of us who would not find that type of rigorous work exhausting.

Some of us feel this way as single people serving in our church. Many of us have been using our spiritual gifts in our churches for years, maybe even decades. But as single people who often feel forgotten in the church, we may wonder why we should keep showing up. As we use the specific gifts that God has given us to help build up, edify, and encourage one another, we may grow tired. When we are weary and frustrated in our singleness, it is important to remember that we work both for the benefit of our spiritual family and for the glory of God, knowing that there is blessing in not giving up.

Paul exhorts the believers in Galatia not to grow weary. He tells them that they will see the fruit of their labor if they do not give up. Moreover, he tells them that their gifts are not for their own benefit or piety but that they should work for the good of all to the glory of God (Galatians 6:9–10).

In our sinful hearts, we might frown at working so diligently for the good of those who may have unknowingly overlooked us in our singleness. We may have needs that have gone unseen, unmet. We may have had our feelings hurt through snide remarks or thoughtless comments made by our brothers and sisters in Christ, who we desperately wish could understand where we are and how we feel. You might be tempted to give up. It can be difficult to continue showing compassion. It is hard to continue to offer forgiveness. It is difficult to continue to give of yourself to people who do not seem to understand you.

But praise God that Jesus did not grow weary and give up. He was misunderstood. He was misused. People called Him names and undermined His purpose, but He did not quit. He knew that He would reap what He sowed. He knew that by sowing suffering, He would reap our salvation. Jesus completed the work that God assigned to Him, not just for His own good but for the good of all—for the whole world.

This exhortation to endure is not an attempt to dismiss your feelings. Your feelings are real, and they are valid. The body of Christ should diligently seek for ways to make everyone feel welcomed and at home. But when you are tempted to give up, look to Jesus. He is the best example that we have for enduring in service to our family in Christ. Patient and gentle, Jesus put aside His own needs, frustrations, and hurts to accomplish something greater. We are like Him when, instead of harboring resentment in our hearts, we choose to love instead.

You—right now—in your singleness have gifts that you can use for the good of the body of Christ. Do not allow your frustrations to keep you from reaping the harvest that is sown when you do not give up. Much like training for an Olympic event, sowing good work is often strenuous and exhausting. You may not even see the full harvest in your lifetime. But know that your service is not in vain. It will produce good fruit for the good of all and glory to the God who gives the harvest.

Patient and gentle, Jesus put aside His own needs, frustrations, and hurts to accomplish something greater.

You — right now — in your singleness have gifts that you can use for *the good of the body of Christ.*

Reflection

How has singleness made you grow weary and want to give up?

What are the benefits of enduring the frustrations of singleness?

No matter who you are or what you have done, *you can have a key to the front door of the kingdom of God.*

You Belong Here: Rahab's Story

JOSHUA 2

The phrase "family of God" sounds pretty weighty. Perhaps it sounds that way because it is true. It *is* weighty. To think that the God of the universe has a family is a sobering reality. God's family is a royal lineage. It is a holy community. It is of a heavenly kingdom. We might think, *It should be hard to find your way in; it should be exclusive . . . right? Who gets to be a part of a family like this?* The profound Old Testament narrative of Rahab shows us that God invites us into His family—regardless of our circumstances or our marital status.

God promised His people, the children of Israel, a land of their own. As this promise peeked over the horizon, the Israelites needed to know more about who currently occupied the land and what they were up against. They sent spies into the land to lay eyes on what was ahead of them.

In the city was Rahab, a prostitute, who knew that God was going to give the land of Canaan to the people of Israel. The Canaanites knew it, too—and they were terrified. Because of this, they panicked, knowing that soon their land would no longer be their own. Having housed the Israelite spies as they were scouting out the land, Rahab begged for mercy for herself and her family. In her pleading, Rahab, who was not even an Israelite, made a profound profession of faith. She believed in Israel's God: "for the Lord your God is God in heaven above and on earth below" (Joshua 2:11).

Because of Rahab's faith, she and her family were spared (Joshua 6:22–25, Hebrews 11:31). Not only did she and her family survive the consequences of the Canaanites's disobedience, Rahab intermarried into Israel.

Often, we only refer to Rahab as the prostitute from the Old Testament. Yet, she became much more than who she was before she placed her faith in the Lord of heaven and earth. In fact, Rahab became a foremother to the Savior. Rahab's faith placed her in the genealogy—the family—of Jesus (Matthew 1:5).

If you think that there is something about you or even your past that would keep you from God's family, take a look at Rahab—foremother of Jesus. Not only was she single at the time she put her faith in the God of Israel, but she bore the shame and pain that came from being a prostitute. Yet, none of this kept her from God's favor. None of this kept God from bringing her into His kindred.

Like we see in Rahab's story, no matter who you are or what you have done, you can have a key to the front door of the kingdom of God. Your singleness does not keep you out. Your past does not keep you out. You do not need a husband or kids of your own to unlock the doors to the Church—you just need faith in Jesus, the Lord of lords.

This is not just a shallow belonging. This is an affiliation that gets recorded in the archives of heaven. And when you are in, you are in for good—there is no fear of being cast out. There is no need to compare yourself to the Christians around you. They are not here because they finally won the prize of a wedding band. They are here by faith, just like you.

This is the goodness of God that is offered to you. This family is on level ground. Whether you marry one day or not at all, whether you ever belong to a husband, you will always belong in this House. By grace, through faith, you will always belong to the family of God.

> *There is no need to compare yourself to the Christians around you.* They are not here because they finally won the prize of a wedding band. They are here by faith, just like you.

By grace, through faith, you will always belong to the family of God.

Reflection

In what ways have you allowed singleness to keep you from identifying with the family of God?

How does being part of God's family provide security in singleness?

In a parched place, *He is a spring of living water.*
His voice assures. His presence soothes.

Seen: Hagar's Story

GENESIS 16, 21:1–22

You might remember the story of Abraham and his wife, Sarah. God promised Abraham that He would make him the father of many nations. But for a long while, the couple (named Abram and Sarai at the time) still had no children. Rather than waiting for God to give them a child, Sarai took the matter into her own hands.

Concerned with the condition of her family tree, Sarai decided that Hagar would be her best option to acquire what she was seeking. If Hagar, Sarai's slave, were to sleep with Sarai's husband Abram, maybe then Sarai and Abram could finally build a family. Just like Eve before her, Sarai took and then gave to her husband (Genesis 3:6). Yet, Hagar was not Sarai's to give. Hagar was not Abram's to have. Nevertheless, she conceived, creating hostility between herself and her mistress, Sarai. Volleyed from Abram's bed to Sarai's bullying, considered no more than property—a means to an end—she fled. But even in devastating circumstances, Hagar found that she was seen and cared for by God—the same God who sees and cares for you.

Like a spring in the wilderness, God appeared to Hagar. In the middle of an unfurling covenant with Abram, God made a promise to bless Hagar and her offspring. God was pleased to receive her gratitude in the form of a title: Hagar's desert designation of the divine is "*El Roi*"—the "God who sees." The Egyptian woman named her baby in remembrance of God's perfect perception of her cries: Ishmael, meaning "God hears."

When the mother and her child were sent away for good this time, God remembered the boy's name. When Ishmael cried out, God heard him weeping under the bush. He provided water for them—the second spring reminding Hagar of the first place where God saw her. Hagar would not be the last exploited woman He would see at a well, speaking a blessing to her bloodline (John 4:1–26).

Like we see in Hagar's story, maybe the people who were supposed to care for you only exacerbated the conditions of your aloneness. Maybe they looked the other way when the abuse happened. Maybe there was no advocate to be found. Maybe you wandered into a torrid desert of despair and doubt.

Sometimes the people who should love us the most wound us the deepest. While you are all by yourself, trying to make it on your own, providing for your children or wondering if you will ever have children of your own, it can seem like no one sees, like no one hears, like no one could ever understand the longing that plagues you day after day.

When the sermons do not feel like they are meant for you; when the emphasis is on other people's children and the matters of their families exclusively; when parishioners see you as only a problem to be solved, a lone sock that cannot find its match; when they do not understand the wounds they create with their words and you are ostracized by their omissions; *El Roi* will meet you here. In a parched place, He is a spring of living water. His voice assures. His presence soothes. He may not always give us what we desire, but He will never turn His back in disinterest.

Jesus knows what it is like to be cast out. He knows what it is like to be misunderstood. Just as God saw Hagar, He sees you. Just as God saw His Son crying out in Gethsemane, His eyes are on you now.

Could the eyes of God in heaven possibly perceive this far? They do.

Behold, the One who beholds you.

Jesus knows what it is like to be cast out. He knows what it is like to be misunderstood. *Just as God saw Hagar, He sees you.*

Behold, the One who *beholds* you.

Reflection

What have you been afraid of in your singleness that you have feared God might not see?

How does Hagar's story reassure you in your singleness?

A Prayer to the God Who Sees

O God, your vision is perfect.
There is nothing that You don't see.
There is nothing that has ever been,
Nothing that has ever existed,
That hasn't crossed Your field of vision.

Have mercy on me, O God,
Your daughter with limited sight.
Forgive me when I forget
That Your eyes don't miss anything,
For when I believe Your sight is set on
Everyone but me.

El Roi
You are the God who sees.

Your eyes are on my loneliness.
Your eyes are on my eyes and the tears they shed.
Your eyes are on my worries.
Your eyes are on my fears.
Your eyes are on my future.

Therefore, I will trust You.
I will trust Your vision
And not mine.

Help me to see what is unseen.
Help me to see what is eternal.

Thank You, God, for seeing;
Not just for seeing,
But for promising,
Not just for promising,
But for your faithfulness.

If there are a million in a room
Your eyes will find me.

Make my eyes
Always see You.

As time bounds closer to heaven,
those who have placed their faith in Jesus
begin to resemble Him more and more.

Just Like Our Father

1 JOHN 3:1–3

Children often resemble their biological parents. Friends, strangers, and family might often comment on which parent the child looks or acts most like. It is natural for children to take on aspects of their parents' character traits or personalities. Some may look or act more like one parent than the other. Some are the perfect combination of both parents. Either way, the genes are present.

We, as brothers and sisters in Christ, now possess the same spiritual DNA as Jesus. As time bounds closer to heaven, those who have placed their faith in Jesus begin to resemble Him more and more. It is easy for us to fix our focus on the differences that we have as believers, especially when it comes to singleness. We compare our lives to the lives of others, and we long to have a reality that looks like theirs. Yet, a day is coming when the lives of all believers will converge into a glorious sameness—whether single or married. We will all be made to look just like our Father.

John teaches us that we are going to be transformed. We are not yet what we will finally be. Though we were all created in the image of God, that image was marred by sin. Now, because of Jesus, we have the hope and promise of existing as God's perfect image again. The completion of this promise is the future that all of God's children await.

Our lives are headed toward a different reality. No matter who we are or what our lives look like right now, we are all being transformed into the same image (2 Corinthians 3:18). When Jesus returns for us, we will be transformed into His likeness and character. Our only concern will be to worship Him and to reflect His glory. Anyone who puts their hope in Jesus should keep this in mind. As His children, we should have our hearts set on being holy as He is holy and pure as He is pure.

Just like a child who reflects the quirks and character traits of her parents, we will look just like our heavenly Father. Your singleness does not change what awaits you in eternity. Though now we may struggle with the annoyances, frustrations, and grief that come along with living life unmarried, we can find comfort in the fact that one day, we will no longer battle those negative feelings. Let the longing you have now for marriage exist at the same time as your longing for heaven. It is okay to hold the two yearnings in tension.

Your singleness is not all that there is. In fact, any hardship that we face now, we will not face forever. Those who are in Christ are promised a life of eternal fellowship with all of the saints in the perfect presence of God. Because Jesus went to the cross, we can have fellowship with Him now and forever. And even more, we will all have the same eternal purpose: to worship and enjoy God forever. No longer will we fixate on what we do not have, for there we will all have everything we have ever needed—Christ Himself.

The whole family will be together. There will be no distinctions between single and married. There will be no loneliness or longing there. We will all be made just like our Father.

Just like a child who reflects the quirks and character traits of her parents, *we will look just like our heavenly Father.*

Because Jesus went to the cross, we can have fellowship with Him *now and forever.*

Reflection

In regard to singleness, how does it encourage you to know that this life is not all that there is?

What does it mean that we will all be like God and transformed into His image?

A Poem of Blessing for the Family of God

FURTHER READING: **Numbers 6:24–26, Hebrews 1:3, Ephesians 2:12–14, 1 Peter 2:9, Ephesians 1:14, Galatians 3:28, Ephesians 2:20–22, Revelation 21:2, Psalm 133:1**

Blessed are you

Those blessed and kept by the Lord

Those who look on the radiance
of God in the face of Jesus

Those who dwell in the Prince of Peace

How beautiful the nations who reside within you

How gorgeous the sound of their praise

You are the perpetual priesthood

You are fortified for fellowship

You are sealed with the Spirit

Let not the dividing walls of hostility

Be resurrected with your hands

Nor the foreigner be banished

Nor the poor pushed out

Nor the sisters silenced

For you are all one

Oh, that the temple would always
yield to the Cornerstone

Oh, that the bride would adorn herself for Him

Oh, that this eternal kindred of
God would dwell in the unity

That was purchased for you on Calvary.

Amen.

"May the LORD bless you
and protect you;
may the LORD make his
face shine on you
and be gracious to you;
may the LORD look with
favor on you
and give you peace.'"

NUMBERS 6:24–26

The gospel compels us to be sanctified,
and in so doing, we are conformed to
the likeness of Christ Himself.

What Is the Gospel?

Thank you for reading and enjoying this booklet with us! We are abundantly grateful for the Word of God, the instruction we glean from it, and the ever-growing understanding it provides for us of God's character. We are also thankful that Scripture continually points to one thing in innumerable ways: the gospel.

We remember our brokenness when we read about the fall of Adam and Eve in the garden of Eden (Genesis 3), where sin entered into a perfect world and maimed it. We remember the necessity that something innocent must die to pay for our sin when we read about the atoning sacrifices in the Old Testament. We read that we have all sinned and fallen short of the glory of God (Romans 3:23) and that the penalty for our brokenness, the wages of our sin, is death (Romans 6:23). We all need grace and mercy, but most importantly, we all need a Savior.

We consider the goodness of God when we realize that He did not plan to leave us in this dire state. We see His promise to buy us back from the clutches of sin and death in Genesis 3:15. And we see that promise accomplished with Jesus Christ on the cross. Jesus Christ knew no sin yet became sin so that we might become righteous through His sacrifice (2 Corinthians 5:21). Jesus was tempted in every way that we are and lived sinlessly. He was reviled yet still yielded Himself for our sake, that we may have life abundant in Him. Jesus lived the perfect life that we could not live and died the death that we deserved.

The gospel is profound yet simple. There are many mysteries in it that we will never understand this side of heaven, but there is still overwhelming weight to its implications in this life. The gospel tells of our sinfulness and God's goodness and a gracious gift that compels a response. We are saved by grace through faith, which means that we rest with faith in the grace that Jesus Christ displayed on the cross (Ephesians 2:8–9). We cannot save ourselves from our brokenness or do any amount of good works to merit God's favor. Still, we can have faith that what Jesus accomplished in His death, burial, and resurrection was more than enough for our salvation and our eternal delight. When we accept God, we are commanded to die to ourselves and our sinful desires and live a life worthy of the calling we have received (Ephesians 4:1). The gospel compels us to be sanctified, and in so doing, we are conformed to the likeness of Christ Himself. This is hope. This is redemption. This is the gospel.

Scriptures to Reference

GENESIS 3:15

I will put hostility between you and the woman, and between your offspring and her offspring. He will strike your head, and you will strike his heel.

ROMANS 3:23

For all have sinned and fall short of the glory of God.

ROMANS 6:23

For the wages of sin is death, but the gift of God is eternal life in Christ Jesus our Lord.

2 CORINTHIANS 5:21

He made the one who did not know sin to be sin for us, so that in him we might become the righteousness of God.

EPHESIANS 2:8–9

For you are saved by grace through faith,
and this is not from yourselves; it is God's gift—
not from works, so that no one can boast.

EPHESIANS 4:1–3

Therefore I, the prisoner in the Lord, urge you to walk worthy of the calling you have received, with all humility and gentleness, with patience, bearing with one another in love, making every effort to keep the unity of the Spirit through the bond of peace.

Your singleness does not change what awaits you in *eternity.*

BIBLIOGRAPHY

Anders, Max. *Galatians-Colossians*. Vol. 8. Holman New Testament Commentary. Nashville, TN: Broadman & Holman Publishers, 1999.

Blum, Edwin A., and Trevin Wax, eds. *CSB Study Bible*: Notes. Nashville, TN: Holman Bible Publishers, 2017.

Bromiley, Geoffrey W., ed. *The International Standard Bible Encyclopedia*, Revised. Wm. B. Eerdmans, 1979–1988.

Elwell, Walter A. *Evangelical Commentary on the Bible*. Vol. 3. Baker Reference Library. Grand Rapids, MI: Baker Book House, 1995.

Matthews, Victor Harold, Mark W. Chavalas, and John H. Walton. *The IVP Bible Background Commentary: Old Testament*. Electronic ed. Downers Grove, IL: InterVarsity Press, 2000.

Merida, Tony. *Exalting Jesus in Ephesians*. Nashville, TN: Holman Reference, 2014.

Thank you for studying God's Word with us!

CONNECT WITH US

@thedailygraceco

@dailygracepodcast

CONTACT US

info@thedailygraceco.com

SHARE

#thedailygraceco

VISIT US ONLINE

www.thedailygraceco.com

MORE DAILY GRACE

Daily Grace® Podcast